Of Love and Other Maladies

A collection of poetry by
Douglas Graham Wilson

Edited by
Lucy Tertia George

Nordville

Cover artwork by Karen Marcus Design
Proofread by Polly Bull

Wordville
www.wordville.net
info@wordville.net

For my grandparents, Alfie and Lorneé
and my mother, Elizabeth.

"There is not one big cosmic meaning for all, there is
only the meaning we each give to our life, an individual
meaning, an individual plot, like an individual novel, a
book for each person."

Anaïs Nin

About Douglas Graham Wilson

 Douglas is a writer and spoken word performer based in London. Originally from Cape Town, his debut performance poetry show was voted one of the Top 10 shows of the year by The Argus Newspaper's entertainment critic Derek Wilson in the arts supplement *Tonight*. He won sponsorship to perform at the Grahamstown Festival and produced numerous solo and collaborative shows throughout the 2000s. Since arriving in the UK, he's been welcomed into the London poetry scene and is a regular at Celine's Salon in Soho.

instagram.com/douglasgrahamwilson

Acknowledgements

Heartfelt thanks to every single person who has encouraged and helped me along this magnificent poetic journey—your belief in my passion inspires me to keep on writing.

Thank you to the multitudes of people who have appreciated and supported my readings and performances across the world for so many years; and a special thanks to my fabulous friend in Cape Town, Bev Johansen, the best MC ever, for all of those stunning introductions.

To all of my fellow poets and bohemians in London town, thank you so much for welcoming me into your magical realm and inspiring me with your brilliant creativity and talent.

A huge thank you to my dearest friend Karen Marcus for the most beautiful cover design.

Celine, I thank my angels for leading me to your Salon—a haven of artistic ingenuity and free expression, underpinned by love and soulfulness.

And to Lucy and Wordville, eternal gratitude for truly seeing, understanding and respecting my work—you've made a lifelong dream a reality and taken my poetry to the next level.

Contents

Lucien in Alabaster

your sensuous movements are exquisite—
fluid, masculine, other-worldly—
as you recline languidly
amongst gossamer grasses.

the evening sun imbues your ivory skin
with light, turning it translucent.

you are magnificent;
a smooth alabaster sculpture
that has come to life beside me.

in the sunset your body shimmers
in and out of invisibility—
as though you're about to transform
into the immortal entity I suspect you are.

your quiet beauty is hypnotising,
enthralling and seducing my senses.

you unexpectedly open your eyes
and turn your head.
your viridescent gaze
disarms,
penetrates,
mesmerises me.

I could worship you.

Love Don't Leave

the writing paper rustles
and blows off the table at dusk,
scattering words and thoughts
upon the floor,
intermingling with freshly
cast
down
lily
petals.

the breeze—
a sigh of conclusion—
quietly pushing
through the patio doors
lifting lace and dust
and welcoming in sunbeams
of golden twilight.

and love,
don't leave him yet,
don't leave him alone and yearning
at sunset,
picking up his feelings
from the floor—
solitary within the beauty
of the closing of another day.

love,
don't leave him yet,
for he has just begun
to understand you.

A Teaspoon of Honey

I take the teaspoon and slide it into his mouth,
past the delicate scarlet of his ripe, supple lips.
the honey flows out upon his tongue,
it forms thick, sweet rivulets over his white teeth
and slowly slides down
like a secret, precious potion.

I take my lips and press them to his.
I feel the warm, wet thrill of his pink persuasion
melting into me
and then I sense the sensuous burst of
the taste of honey and the taste of him.

I take my tongue
and slide it deeper into him
and at that moment
his soul is mine—
completely.

The Field

standing in a field
of endless outstretched green
bordered by bare trees,
their plaintive branches
reaching upwards towards an impassive dove-grey sky,

standing there, silently
momentarily lost or abandoned,
with thoughts swirling, twirling within the wind;

pain or a momentary loss of meaning
can sometimes begin to soar
like the haphazard flight of birds,
ravens that appear on the horizon,
coal-black and raucous against the pale.

and solitude can be fragile,
sometimes weak and confounding
or overwhelming perhaps.

and as the abandonment grows
so too the sinister flock multiplies,
relentlessly flapping and teaming
until the sky,
the field,
the bordering trees,
can no longer
be perceived.

so many wings and sharp beaks and claws
and dark soulless eyes,
a hurricane swirling and scratching,
an avalanche of feathery musings
that defile any sense of perspective.

there is nothing else to do
but wait it out,
wait for the marauding tangle to pass,
with all of its squawking and cruel bustle
until
finally
the sky reappears,
and the expansive field
and the bordering trees with their brittle beauty.

then just to stand,
just to stand and breathe
and regain balance.

to regain belief
and then to walk away from it all.

Undertow

I happened upon a woman
staring out across the swirling river
holding a glass of wine absentmindedly—
a wreath of roses and chrysanthemums beside her.

the poignancy of her sorrow was arresting,
compelling me to stop and sit,
a little distance from her.

we sat together in silence
for a long time
watching the Thames slide by.

finally
she stood to go,
and then there we were:
a half-finished glass of wine,
a funeral wreath
and me—
abruptly abandoned on a stone wall.

I touched the taut white and orange petals lightly—
they looked so cheerful in their macabre little circle,
but they belonged beside a grave.

at last
I flung the wreath into the river,
liberating both of us.

Perishing Petals

that tulip
staring me right in the face,
on a sinister, bent stem—
half inquisitive,
half threatening,
with a deep, black heart
sinking and plunging
into places I don't even
want to know about.

and that mean little yellow
goat's head
inside,
in the centre,
stirring up restlessness.

and all is silent in the room,
the tulip and I,
both with dead still heads,
both bending towards
the inevitable.

A Walk through Regent's Park

today I encountered
the ghost of a former self.
he was following me,
darting surreptitiously
among groomed flower beds,
hiding behind trees.

his presence was startling,
evoking wistful memories and emotions
long buried.

I pretended to be unaware
so as not to scare him off,
hoping that he'd draw near
and come more clearly into focus.

tentatively, he approached
becoming less amorphous
as he emerged from between the shadows.

I was struck by his youthful fragility,
suddenly remembering the summer
I had brought him here years ago—
those beautiful afternoons
spent alone,
running and thinking and crying
along these dappled avenues.

I greeted him ardently,
"hello, it's been a while."
he remained silent,
stepping out into the sunlight
to hold me.

the past and present merged—
aspects of one soul
peacefully re-assimilated
and unified
again.

A Deep Blue Truth

take the stone,
throw the stone
far across the lake.
observe the ripples
as they form shockwaves within its wake.
then watch the gentle water flowers
shudder with the chant—
moving liquid,
liquid energy
making all form slant.

then
touch an angel's weeping eye,
place your finger within that space
and see his beautiful tears
turn to holiness upon his face.
choose goodness, freedom,
hope and love.
let your heart shimmer like gold—
call out to your creator,
to the winds above
and watch your precious soul
grow bold.

Night Sky

tonight the clouds are
electric blue puffs of smoke
from God's Havana.

Decomposition

I feel the touch of imminent freedom
against my cheek
and the soft caress flows
into my heart,
sending a waterfall of liquid light
plummeting
into my soul;
that eternal aspect of my being
contained within the fragile shell of my mortality—
this throbbing biological mechanism
engineered by celestial scientists.

and how perplexing it is
to journey through this expanse,
perceiving the faint and intermittent resonance
of deeper truths
transmitted like Morse code
from stars and orbs
hanging within a limitless cosmos,
like words whispered and lost
on a deathbed.

our lives swirl through the atmosphere,
carried as haphazardly as leaves
in autumn winds,
blowing toward hidden destinies—
the brittle expressions
of our eternal shapes and forms
that glide above us,
transparent doppelganger puppeteers,
manipulating the invisible strings
that connect humanity
and make us one.

I feel the heat of silent words
uttered above my skull;
secret, silvery vapours
that creep across my forehead
and then condense upon it
like a baptismal blessing.

in the distance she beckons to me silently—
the woman in white—
her thin arm extended
in a plaintive gesture
of sinister skeletal elegance
alluding to transience and transmutation.

and we grow and bloom with innocent passion,
germinating from a transcendental will.
ephemeral beings from another realm
temporarily trapped within three dimensions.
static electricity,
translucent ectoplasm,
imperishable stardust,
condensed galactic molecules
waiting to be released.

ETHAN

"I do not wish to continue this conversation,"
you said.
well then, don't.
you stood up,
walked over to the window
and stared at the sea.
I watched you,
looking for a sign.

rubbing the smooth arm of the couch,
I stood up.
I could feel the rush of blood
from standing
flushing my lips and cheeks.
you turned to look at me,
then quickly turned away
to stare at the ocean again.

the wind picked up
as I poured myself a scotch.
the imposing silence of the room
began shrieking through cracks
between the window frames and doors.

"do you think you can forgive me?" you asked.
I looked at a photograph,
running my fingers through my hair,
sighing quietly as I stroked the golden picture frame.
the telephone rang
and I waited for you to answer it.
you didn't.
I didn't.
it stopped.

the sky was clouding over,
the light ochre,
touched with gold;
it was a beautiful afternoon.
I walked over to the couch
and sat down again,
crossing my legs and then uncrossing them.

you were still at the window looking at the sea.
"I don't want to lose you," you said.
I knew you meant it.
I thought how good the scotch tasted,
how comfortable the couch was
and how nice your new shoes looked
lying over there on the carpet.
I didn't answer you.

you left the room,
I stood up slowly
and walked to where you had been standing.
I could smell the fragrance of you.
I looked at your view—
it was melancholy
like us.
the water was becoming turbulent
in the strong winds,
the clouds dark and imposing.
no tears came out of my eyes—
in fact, they felt very dry.

I could hear you in the kitchen,
could smell the lemon and ginger tea.
why was this happening to us?
I allowed the reality of the situation
to enter,
and then you came back into the room.
"I know you don't believe me," you said,
"it meant nothing.
it's over.
it's done."
your words echoed.

"yes, it's done,"
I finally answered.

you came up behind me,
put your warm hands on my shoulders
and pressed your chest against my back.
"I'm going to leave now,"
you whispered into my ear.
I kept staring through the window.
you picked up your car keys,
I felt you hesitate.
my mouth was parched—
I wanted to swallow the words.

it began to rain,
as you left.

THE REALISATiON

a brooding expression emanates
from behind your eyes
as you lie on your side facing me.

I can never figure out what you're thinking—
you hide your emotions so well.

all I'm ever able to detect is
a sort of constant, nagging antipathy
that's barely perceptible,
flickering across your face.

your unease
confounds me.

you roll away without saying a word,
lifting yourself from the bed, sighing.

turning your head coolly
on that slender marble neck of yours,
you look back at me
with a detached expression—
nonchalant as a breeze.

and right then I realise:
you don't love me anymore.
you probably never did.

Love at Long Distance

and as I ran through the night
I sang songs to exorcise your spirit
but the cold wind
blew away the melody,
blew my words
back into my mouth.

and the Moon seemed so lonely
up there in the sky,
with the huge, fat reflections
of Venus and Mars
pulsating below
its sickle and shadow
from so far away.

and I passed the spirit trunks of tall trees
waving me by,
waving me away
from their secret dance,
with the freezing breath of
night air.

and I was an intruder out there,
as I felt within myself.
and so
I descended the terrace stairs,
blown like torn silk,
inadequate and small
amidst the passion of night.

a place few explore,
a danger to enter into;
a place that can only emphasise
the irony of life
and the torture of being apart.

Musings of a Nemophilist

perhaps I wanted to be
like the rocks in forest streams,
rounded and smooth
and covered in green moss.
maybe that's what I wished to be—
stoic, yet soft and sure,
in the same place every day,
resting below a canopy of trees,
dappled sunlight shining down
upon my glistening surfaces
snugly wedged in clay,
basking in the coolness,
the stillness
 —a rock—
safely anchored and caressed
by the passing spirits of the forest—
those who would come to find respite
where I lived.
that's probably what I was imagining,
coaxed by watery glinting
and seduced by leafy tranquillity.
but I changed my musing
and transmuted myself into a stream instead.
sparkling fluidity
lured by gravity
upon a rapid and mysterious journey
rushing down,
down,
down,
toward an unknown destiny,
smoothing rocks along the way.
perhaps I wanted to be of the forest,
serene and furtive and soft,
forever concealed below cool shadows.
yes, that's what I wished to be.

Melancholia

yes,
that lazy feeling of gloom,
the sly little emotion
who hides behind songs
and memories in your head.

do you know him?
that secretive gargoyle who cuddles
into the warm, blood-red corner
of your heart,
making you feel
all languid and intoxicated—
who shows you a landscape
of arum lilies and Gothic castles
and clothes you
in soft white robes
within misty forest clearings.

have you heard him singing
to you
in his melodic, maledictive voice?
singing songs about lost love
and life's bittersweet pains.
he has the ability to remain
a tolerable guest
within the realm of your feelings,
doesn't he?

A Shattered Heart

how I yearn
for the soul of my soul;
for the deep recognition that will flow
between us
when we finally
discover each other.
how I yearn
for the soft
love that will blossom
when at last
we meet.

it would be an evil compromise
to settle for anything but
our highest hopes
for true love.

and so,
it is a quiet path of solitude
I choose for now—
until that moment
when, perhaps,
time will turn into timelessness.

we shatter when discarded
by reckless paramours
in the quest for devotion—
yet, our fragmented hearts
expand in readiness.

true love, it is a noble feat—
one that requires the courage
to face and heal the pain
that has ripped you apart
and yet—
despite the tearing—
made you more beautiful.

Lightning Source UK Ltd.
Milton Keynes UK
UKHW021319230222
399123UK00006B/232